"I may not be a lion
But I am a lion's cub
And I have a lion's heart"

Elizabeth 1

For Charlotte

whose curiosity about real queens
was the inspiration for this book

© 2025 by Jennifer Johnston

All rights reserved.

No portion of this book may be reproduced in any form without written permission from the publisher or author.

The Queens Alphabet

Meet real queens from history

A is for Artemisia II (Ah-ti-mee-zia) of the Kingdom of Caria in Persia

She built a tomb for her husband, King Mausolus.

It was so pretty that it was made one of the Seven Wonders of the World.

It was called a mausoleum.

Lived to be 44 years old

395 BC - 351 BC

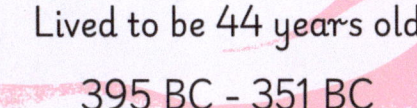

daisy

She used plants from the daisy family to create medicines.

These statues are copies of ancient statues of Artemisia II and Mausolus.

'Bodrum, sochy Hérodota, Artemísia a Mausóla' by Mickapr via wikimedia commons is licensed under CC BY 4.0 Cropped from original

B is for
Boudicca (Boo-di-kah)
of the Iceni (Eh-kane-i) Tribe in Britain

After her husband died the Romans in Britain treated her and her daughters terribly.

So she called upon the people in Britain to help her attack the Romans and to force them out of Britain.

She won five battles and set London on fire. In the sixth and final battle she was finally defeated.

Lived to be 31 years old
30 AD - 61 AD

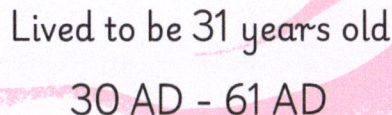 bluebell

Albert Kretschmer was a German professor, painter, costume researcher, and he was the director of the Theatre in Berlin.

This drawing of Boudicca is from his book 'Costumes of All Nations'.

'Queen Boudicea (Boudicca) of the ancient British Iceni tribe' by Albert Kretschmer via Wikimedia Commons, CC BY 4.0

C is for Cleopatra of Egypt

She was beautiful and she was clever. She learnt about maths and science, and she knew how to speak at least seven different languages.

Out of her family she was the only one who could speak Egyptian.

The old historian Plutarch wrote that she had a sweet voice and could be a very persuasive person.

Lived to be 39 years old
70 BC - 30 BC

blue lotus

The glamourous actress Claudette Colbert posing as Cleopatra for the movie in 1934.

'Cleopatra Publicity Photo' by Paramount Studios via wikimedia commons, public domain

D is for Dihya (D'hee-ah)

of the Kingdom of Aurès (Or-res) in Algeria

A Berber Warrior Queen, who was described 'a true desert woman' and 'an excellent rider and a shooter who never misses'*.

She fought an army to keep her people free. Not only that, she then chased that army, captured Carthage, the city they had run to, and became the ruler there.

*by historian Nahum Slouschz

Lived to be 35 years old
668 AD - 703 AD

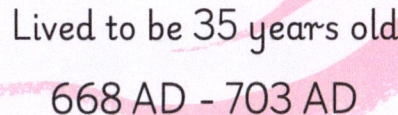

iris

National flower of Algeria.

A statue of Dihya in the city Khenchela in Algeria.

By ⵜⴰⵎⴰⵣⵉⵖⵜ
date approx 2022, from Google Images

E is for Elizabeth I of England

Her reign is known as 'The Golden Age' of England.

Spain had sent ships to invade England, and the English ships tried to stop them.

Elizabeth wore a white dress with armour, and she rode a white horse to give a speech to uplift her soldiers.

Lived to be 69 years old

1533 AD - 1603 AD

Tudor rose

The symbol of the Tudor kings and queens, who ruled England for over one hundred years.

This painting celebrated the defeat of the Spanish Armada in 1588.

It is called the 'Armada Portrait'.

'Elizabeth I (Armada Portrait)' formerly attributed to George Gower (1540-1596) from Woburn Abbey Collection via Wikimedia Commons, Public Domain, cropped from original

F is for Fredegund (Fred-ah-g'nd) of Soissons (Swa-son), France

To win a battle she had her soldiers carry large tree branches in the night for them to hide while they walked.

This clever plan may have been Shakespeare's inspiration for the 'moving' Birnam Wood in his play 'MacBeth'.

Lived to be 50 years old
547 AD - 597 AD

hydrangea

King Chilperic married Queen Fredegund, who was his third wife.

She continued to reign as queen after he was killed by a mysterious stranger while he was out hunting.

'CHILPERIC 1er ET FREDEGONDE' from Jean Du Tillet, 16th Century, from Wikimedia Commons, Public Domain

G is for Guinevere (Gwen-ah-veer) of Britain

She was a very beautiful lady, a legendary queen who married King Arthur.

She had her own seat at the Round Table with King Arthur and the brave Sir Lancelot, and all the other noble knights.

Lived into her later years in a nunnery
5th or 6th Century

Snowdrop

'Guinevere'
By Henry Ford, 1910

By Henry Justice Ford (1860-1941) - The Leicester Galleries loans to The Speed Art Museum, Луисвилл, Кентукки, Wikimedia Commons, Public Domain

H is for Hatshepsut (Hat-shep-soot) of Egypt

She made herself into a powerful Pharaoh. She often dressed as a man and she would wear a fake beard.

Hatshepsut had her men go out in ships, they explored and found great treasures in the Land of Punt.

Lived to be either 37 or 47 years old
1505 or 1495 BC - 1458 BC

bird of paradise

This statue of Hatshepsut shows her wearing the Nemes headdress of the Pharaohs.

'Seated Statue of Hatshepsut MET' from Metropolitan Museum of Art, via Wikimedia Commons, Public Domain

I
is for
Isabella I of Castile in Spain

Isabella gave a man named Christopher Columbus her royal blessing and money to help him to travel to and explore America, which was called 'The New World'.

The Spanish people began to live in this 'New World', and so the Spanish Golden Age began.

Lived to be 53 years old

1451 AD - 1504 AD

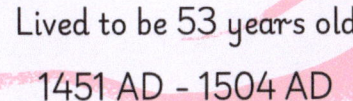
blue pimpernel

Isabella is wearing a gold necklace with a pendent made with rubies and pearls.

'Isabella I of Spain (1451-1504)' from Hampton Court Palace Royal Collection, via Wikimedia Commons, Public Domain

J is for Jane Grey of England

When the king died Mary, his daughter, was meant to be queen, but an important man quickly made Mary's cousin, Lady Jane Grey, the queen instead.

In nine days Mary came with an army. She put Jane in prison in the Tower and then became queen.

Lived to be 17 years old

1537 AD - 1554 AD

english rose

In this picture Jane Grey is wearing a black dress and a black headpiece.

She is holding a book which might be a bible or a prayer book.

'Lady Jane Grey Painting' from Audley End House Collection, Essex, via Wikimedia Commons, Public Domain

K
is for

Keladi Chennamma
(Ke-lah-di Che-na-mah)

of Karnataka in India

She very bravely protected and gave shelter to another king as he was running from his enemy.

She did this even though she knew that the king he was running away from would now fight against her, too.

Reigned for 25 years
Died in 1696 AD

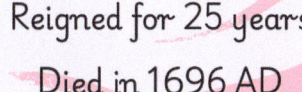
Parakeet flower

The people of Karnataka preferred her leadership over that of her husband, the king. So, in 1671, they crowned Keladi as queen.

From that moment on, she—not the king—would rule the kingdom.

Medium.com 'A Durga a day: Day 3-Mata Chandraghanta: Keladi Rani Chennamma' by Shivara S, 13 October 2018 https://medium.com/@surashiva/a-durga-a-day-day-3-mata-chandraghanta-keladi-rani-chennamma-f83baf9f4883, cropped from original

$\mathcal{L}$ is for Lili'uokalani (Lili Oh-kah-lah-nee) of Hawaii

Lili'uokalani was the only queen Hawaii ever had. She made a new constitution, an important law.

Some people from America didn't like it, so they came and took control of the Kingdom of Hawaii instead.

Aloha 'Oe (Oy), a beautiful song, was a good-bye song that she wrote.

Lived to be 79 years old
1838 AD - 1917 AD

Pua kalaunu

Lili'uokalani would wear this flower in her hair and in leis.

Photo by Carol VanHook, CC BY-SA 2.0 via Wikimedia Commons

Lili'uokalani at Queen Victoria's Golden Jubilee in 1887.

That was four years before she became Hawaii's queen.

'Liliuokalani in London' from Hawaii State Archives, via Wikimedia Commons, Public Domain

M

is for

Marie Antoinette
(Mah-ree An-twa-net)

of France

Her home was in the Palace of Versailles (Ver-sigh).

People in France were very poor, cold and hungry, but they could see how rich the royals were. So they decided they didn't want a king or queen to rule them anymore.

She was the last Queen of France before the time of the brutal French Revolution.

Lived to be 37 years old

1755 AD - 1793 AD

Peony

'Marie Antoinette with a rose'

By Élisabeth-Louise Vigée Le Brun in 1783.

From Palace of Versailles Collection, Google Arts and Culture, Public Domain

N is for Nefertiti of Egypt

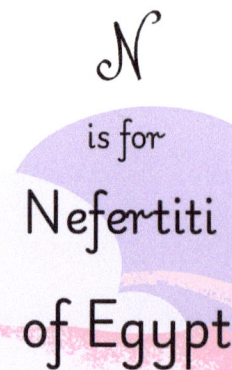

Her name means that 'a beautiful woman has come'.

She was the Great Royal Wife of the Pharoah.

Together they told people to worship Aten, the sun disk, as their God.

Lived to be 40 years old
1370 BC - 1330 BC

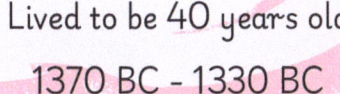 jasmine

A painted limestone bust of Nefertiti.

'Nofretete Neues Museum' by Philip Pikart, 8 Nov 2009, from Neues Museum Berlin, via Wikimedia Commons, licensed under CC BY 3.0

O is for Otrera (Aw-tree-rah) of the Amazons

Greek legends say she was the very first Queen of the Amazons.

The Amazons were all girls who were great fighters.

Otrera trained the women in her village to fight, then they killed the boys.

Later on she married the Greek God of War, Ares.
(Air-rees)

A demigoddess
Greek Bronze Age

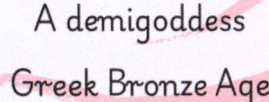
everlasting

A painting of a Greek fighting an Amazon on a sarcophagus in Italy from 350-325 BC.

'Produzione greca o magnogreca, sarcofago delle amazzoni, 350-325 a.C. ca, da tarquinia 05' by Sailko, 1 January 2014 via Wikimedia Commons, licensed under CC BY 3.0

P is for

Paccha Duchicela
(Pa-cha Doo-chi-sel-ah)

of the Inca Empire

She grew up as a princess and then became queen of the Kingdom of Quito.

Quito became part of the massive Inca Empire and she married the Inca Emperor.

It is said that she had four children, and one of them may have been the last Inca Emperor before the Spanish came.

Lived to be 40 years old
1485 AD - 1525 AD

cantuta

A sacred flower for the Inca people.

Artwork of Paccha Duchicela from 1933.

The text says 'Queen of Quito and Puruhá'.

'Paccha Duchicela' by Satrap Photo from Archivo Nacional de Fotografía de Ecuador via Wikimedia Commons, Public Domain

Q is for Queen

A baby princess who is born 'next in line' in the Royal Family can become queen.

She is called a **Queen Regnant.**

A lady can be a queen if she is married to a King.

She is called a **Queen Consort**.

R
is for

Ranavalona (Rah-nah-vah-loo-nah)
of Madagascar

People who were from England and France had come. They wore different types of clothes, and they began to teach her people new ideas.

Ranavalona did what she needed to do so that she could keep her country the same.

She didn't want it to change.

Lived to be 83 years old

1778 AD – 1861 AD

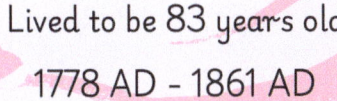

darwin's orchid

'Ranavalona I'

'Ranavalona I' by Philippe-Auguste Ramanankirahina (1860-1915) dated 1905 from Lapan' Andafiavaratra (Antananarivo) via Wikimedia Commons, Public Domain

S
is for
Shajar al-Durr
of Egypt

Shajar married the Sultan, who was the ruler of Egypt.

When he died she was the Sultan for about three months.

In those three months the King of France and his army, who had been captured, agreed to give her lots and lots of money to be able to go home.

Lived to be 37 years old
1220 AD - 1257 AD

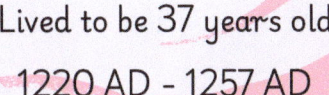
daffodil

Shajar al-Durr's Tomb in Cairo, Egypt.

It was likely she had it built in 1250.

'Mausoleum of Shajar al-Durr' by R Prazeres, 8 June 2019, via Wikimedia Commons, licensed under CC BY 4.0

T is for Toyo (Tow-yow) of Japan

Japan had had a great queen. After she died there was a King who was so terrible that Japan's people just wanted a girl to be their Queen again.

Toyo, who was 13 years old, was the next girl in line to replace that King and to be the Queen of Japan.

Born in 235 AD

cherry blossom

A portrait of Japanese Empress Suiko which was made by using coloured silk.

She was an Empress in Japan about 300 years after Toyo.

'Empress Suiko' by Tosa Mitsuyoshi, 1726, Eifuku-ji temple, Osaka, Yahoo Japan, via Wikimedia Commons, Public Domain

U
is for
Ulrika Eleonora
of Denmark

Ulrika was very kind and she was generous, and loved to help others. She liked to paint and draw.

She was going to marry the King of Sweden, but a war between Denmark and Sweden meant that the wedding was cancelled. Years went by and finally she was able to marry the King of Sweden.

Lived to be 36 years old

1656 AD - 1693 AD

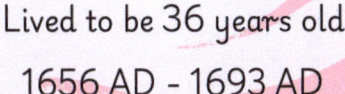
red clover

She is holding a spruce shoot in her hand, to symbolise growth.

At the time she was pregnant with her first child.

'Ulrika Eleonora of Sweden' by David Klöcker Ehrenstrahl, 1686, via Wikimedia Commons, Public Domain

V is for Victoria of England

Dash was her pet Spaniel, and her friend. She called him "dear sweet little Dash".

She was just eighteen when she became the queen.

The years when Victoria was the queen are known as 'The Victorian Era'.

Lived to be 81 years old

1819 AD – 1901 AD

violet

A special flower for Victoria as her husband would give her violets.

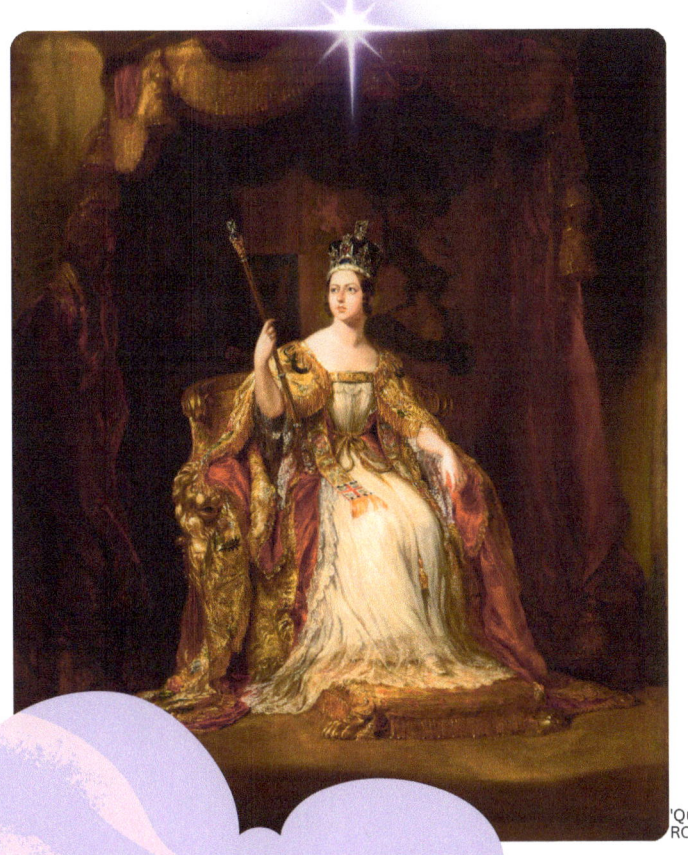

A painting of Queen Victoria at her coronation.

Although she became queen as soon as the last king died, the coronation was a special ceremony where she was crowned and officially made Queen of England.

'Queen Victoria' by George Hayter, 1838, Royal Collection RCIN 401213, via Wikimedia Commons, Public Domain

W is for Wilhelmina of the Netherlands

Every day during World War II she used the radio to talk to the people who were in her country.

Hearing her voice each day helped to give her people hope to survive the war.

Lived to be 82 years old
1880 AD – 1962 AD

tulip

Queen Wilhelmina abdicated after being queen for 50 years.

This means she gave up the crown, and her daughter Juliana became the new queen.

'Queen Wilhelmina & Juliana' circa 1914 from Bain Collection, via Wikimedia Commons, Public Domain

X is for Xiuhtlaltzin (Shee-oot-lahl-tzeen)
of the Toltec Empire, Mexico

Her name means 'Flower of the Little Earth'.

She ruled as a wonderful, good and wise queen. When she died she was buried in the Temple of the Frog God.

Reigned for 4 years
after her husband died

She died in 983 AD

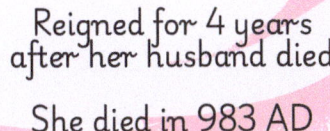 marigold

Digital artwork of the Toltec Queen.

'Toltec Queen Xiuhtzaltzin' by Miguel Angel Omaña Rojas, 2022,
via Wikimedia Commons, licensed under CC BY 4.0

Y
is for
Yoko (Yow-kow)
of the Mende People in Sierra Leone

Madam Yoko was a wise and clever leader and warrior.

She used the river system to help to protect the villages from attacks.

Lived to be 57 years old
1849 AD - 1906 AD

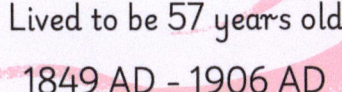

african tulip tree

Madam Yoko is wearing a medal that was given to her by Queen Victoria.

University of Aberdeen 'Madam Yoko's Snuff Box and Collections from Sierre Leone' by Richard Anderson 21 October 2021
https://www.abdn.ac.uk/collections/blog/madam-yokos-snuff-box-and-collections-from-sierra-leone/

Z is for
Zenobia (Zen-oh-bia)
of the Palmyrene (Pal-my-reen) Empire in Syria

As the Queen she freed her kingdom from the Romans, and then went on to conquer Egypt.

She was the queen for five years.

Eventually she was captured by the Romans.

Lived to be 34 years old
240 AD - 274 AD

persian cyclamen

'Zenobia In Chains'

by Harriet Goodhue Hosmer in 1859.

'Zenobia in Chain - front view - HLAMBG', photo by Eric Polk, 13 July 2023 at Huntington Library, Art Museum, and Botanical Garden, San Merino, California, USA, via Wikimedia Commons, Public Domain

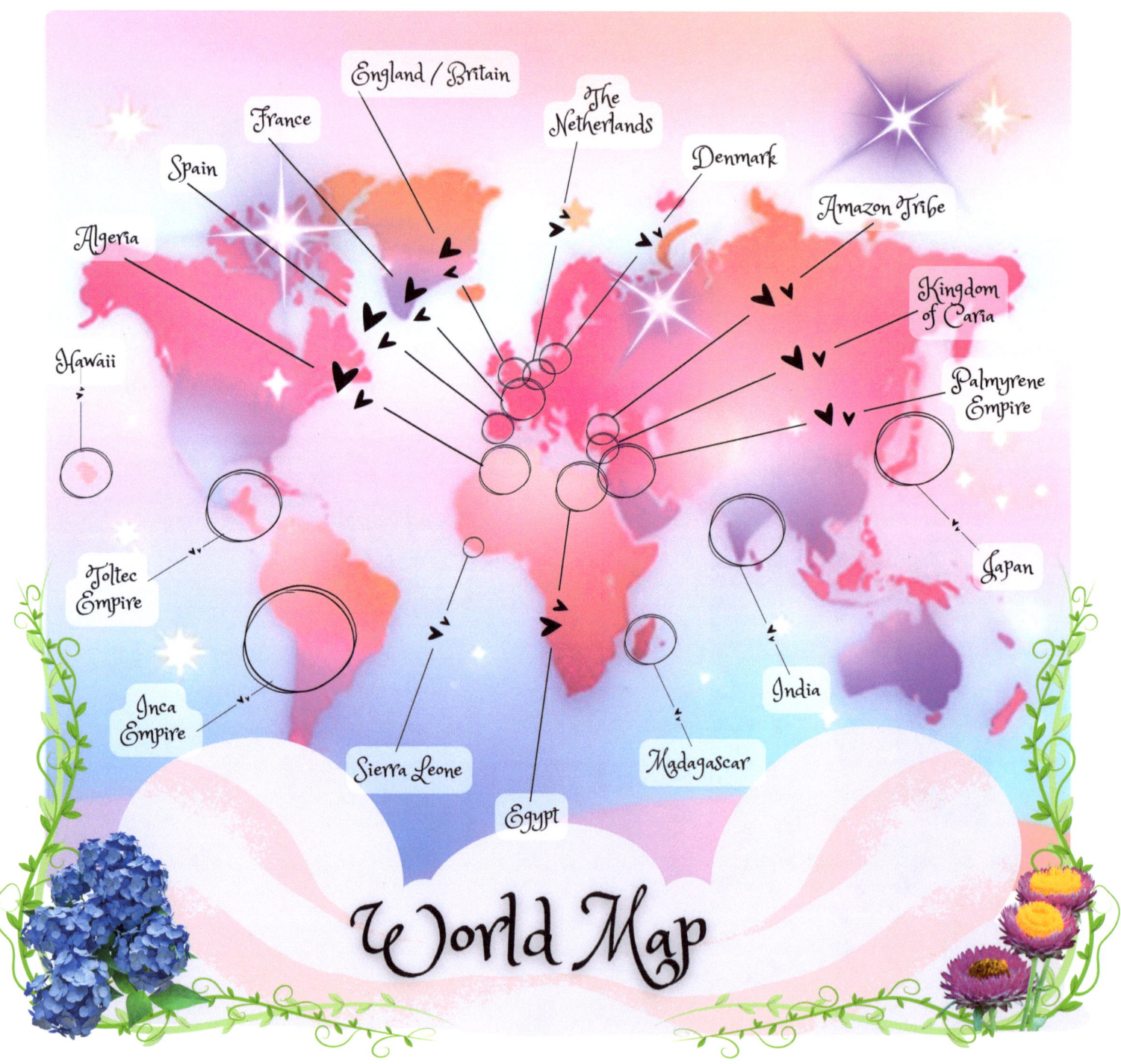